Real Homeschool

Letting Go of the
Pinterest-Perfect
and
Instagram-Ideal Homeschool

by Karen DeBeus

Please visit me at
www.simplylivingforhim.com
and join me as we encourage each other
to live more simply
for the glory of God.

Simply Living…for Him

A NOTE TO READERS:

This book is a collection of my thoughts and convictions on so many things that influence our homeschools. I am not asking for my thoughts to be your thoughts or my convictions to be your convictions.

Please, always let your convictions be between you and God. As I always tell people,

"Don't listen to me... Listen to GOD."

He is the one you ultimately answer to and follow. Glean what you can from my thoughts. If you agree, wonderful! Let's chat some more! If you don't, wonderful! He has you on a different journey! We can still chat some more!

I am not trying to change anyone, but to gently whisper words of encouragement and share where I have felt God leading me in my life. We should all be searching scripture as our main basis.

I never claim to know it all or even to know very much! Ha! I am just a homeschooling mom, who by God's grace has been given a voice to reach others. I intend to use that voice to honor Him as best as I can.

Thank you for reading my words, and I pray that in some way they bless you.

Blessings and joy,

Karen

Acknowledgments

First and foremost, my thanks go to my Lord and Savior Jesus Christ, *who brought me out of the pit of mud and mire and set my feet on a rock (Psalm 40)! Without Him, I am nothing, and with Him the possibilities are endless (John 15:5, Matthew 19:26).*

It is my prayer to do everything for His Glory. Less of me, and more of Him.

I also want to thank my amazing husband and love of my life; my four beautiful children who have exceeded my dreams beyond my wildest imagination; and my parents, sister, and in-laws who love me no matter what and accept me for who I am and for who I have become on this journey.

And finally, I'm grateful to all of those in the amazing homeschooling community out there whose love and support these past several years are much appreciated.

The encouragement I have received for this book, while in the writing stages, is deeply appreciated. I have met so many beautiful families on this journey. I pray every word honors God.

A special thank you to Linda Singerle. God sent her to me at just the right time. I am extremely grateful for her expertise and work to edit this book.

Introduction — Don't Skip This Part!

Whenever I read a book, I have a tendency to skip the introduction and dive right into the book. I hope you will not do that and will read this because it sets up the hows and whys of this book.

This book is not really about social media per se, but more about our hearts in a world that continues to push us to be more like it. Everywhere we turn, social media is screaming at us and showing us pictures of what we should be. Slowly, gradually, we start following the world and trying to bring God with us, rather than letting God lead us and then bringing the world with *us!*

This year we will begin our 10th year of homeschooling, which is nothing short of a miracle, considering I never thought of homeschooling until I was there registering my daughter for kindergarten at the local public school. It has been truly a journey, and we are taught by the Lord each and every minute. I am eternally grateful.

I began writing about halfway into my homeschooling journey; first it was a hobby and a way to share with my family and friends. I started a little online journal, which was called Beautiful Feet Bring Good News. I would share what we were learning in our homeschool and the fun things we were doing. The blog existed mainly so I could let my family and friends see that we really *were* learning at home since many had been opposed to our decision. I didn't even know that other people were reading blogs back then!

Well, that little online journal soon became a blog that other people *were* reading, and soon I was writing for various publications. Out of that little journal came my blog, Simply Living for Him, which to this day remains my heart and ministry to write about simplifying all areas of our lives, including homeschooling, so that we can limit the distractions that take away our focus from God.

About five years ago, I wrote this little book called Simply Homeschool: Have Less Clutter and More Joy in Your Homeschool. I had been speaking about simplifying homeschool, and I turned my presentation into this short eBook. I really didn't think anyone would read it, but once again God amazed me when it became a #1 best-seller on Amazon. Since then, I have written Called Home: Finding Joy in Letting God Lead

Your Homeschool, and Simply Homeschool 2nd Edition. Both have remained on Amazon's best-seller lists. It has been an incredible journey to be able to share the words of my heart with others. Only to God be the glory!

I pray over every single word I write. I always want the message to honor the Lord and to please Him. This past year God laid the idea for this book on my heart and it just wouldn't leave until I started writing it. I prayed the entire time that I wrote this book, all the while making sure it was His will. He kept leading me to write it, even when I had my doubts or challenges. I pray this message touches others on their homeschooling journey and encourages them to keep their focus on God.

What Is a Real Homeschool?

I have seen some amazing changes in the homeschooling community in the past few years. Many of them have been positive, and I truly love being part of this beautiful community of like-minded people.

However, some of the changes are a little concerning. I have seen them in myself, and I have worked to nip them in the bud. I also have to work to keep them from coming back.

They are the desires that creep in and take my focus off of my true purpose in homeschooling. You know what I mean— when the focus becomes all about finding the best curriculum or filling up the schedule with the most extracurricular activities? Or how about decorating the perfect homeschool room? Or the hours spent online searching what others are doing, while neglecting your own time with the Lord? These are all things that have become an issue with me, and I am sure with others, especially as social media grows.

I have often thought about those early homeschoolers who had no Internet or fancy curriculum but truly sought the Lord in their decision to homeschool. I admire them so much! They weren't busy showing off their schoolrooms or their kids on Instagram; they were deep in the nitty-gritty of daily homeschool life when homeschooling wasn't even mainstream. They weren't spending hours on Pinterest, but probably hours in the Word.

This book will challenge us to get back to the basics and fully rely on God. We need to stop living up to an Internet ideal and live only for God's ideals. This book isn't at all a book against social media (after all, I work in social media), but more about our hearts and what we do *with* social media. Pinterest and Instagram and all the other media out there are certainly not bad in and of themselves, but we do need to be aware of our hearts when using them. We must not let those things rule our standards. Only God should rule us.

Since I work in social media, I feel the responsibility to use it well and to use it for good. Hopefully, through this book and my writing and speaking, we can change the way we view the Internet and worldliness in our homeschools.

Will you join me as we get back to the basics? Will you join me as we endeavor to be *real* with each other because we need each other? Will you join me as we focus on what God wants for our homeschools and not what the world says is success?

Will you join me as we pursue **Real Homeschool?** Not a picture-perfect homeschool, but a **real homeschool** – where the rubber meets the road and it sometimes gets messy –and we work together through those messes…

And then it gets beautiful…oh, so beautiful…because God is right there with us. He is working through our families on this real homeschooling journey.

God has called us to this beautiful journey…and the perfect picture is the one where He is leading every step, guiding us, and our eyes are fixed solely on Him.

REAL HOMESCHOOL

A real homeschool is one with God at the center.

A real homeschool is the one where He is glorified.

A real homeschool may not look beautiful on the outside, but on the inside, the heart work is being done and the Lord is working.

A real homeschool is one where mommies are lifting each other up in a beautiful community and not competing with each other.

A real homeschool is being transformed by Him and not conforming to this world.

Let's get rid of the "Pinterest-Perfect" and the "Instagram Ideal" and get back to His ideal. He is the only perfect we need. Let us take this road together…and be real.

Real Homeschool.
It is a beautiful picture.

Chapter 1

Real Ideals

Good-Bye Pinterest-Perfect and Instagram-Ideal

Focus on God's Ideals

We have all been there. It's midnight, and we are endlessly scrolling through Pinterest. What started out as a simple thought–

"Maybe I can find a good idea on Pinterest!"

–has turned into a three-hour marathon of scrolling and searching. We jump from one pin and one website to the next and before we know it, we have forgotten what we even started out looking for. We endlessly scroll in search of something but never really find it.

There is, however, one thing we have managed to find on Pinterest.

Discontentment.

We went from searching idea after idea into a downward spiral that ended in self-pity and dissatisfaction.

"Wow, this mom really has it all together."

"Wow, what a beautiful homeschool room."

"Wow, all of their kids are smiling *all of the time.*"

"Wow, they have it *all.*"

Homeschooling is about so much more than a snapshot of a day; it is a lifelong journey. It is about education, discipleship, family, and eternal matters. We are shaping a whole new generation in a countercultural way. Discipleship has nothing to do with a fancy schoolroom or cutesy arts and crafts. This journey is much more serious. The future is at stake.

We need to stop.

We need to stop getting distracted. If we are distracted by worldly things, before we know it, we will have shifted from our eternal perspective to a worldly one. We cannot emphasize the temporal instead of the eternal. We must keep our focus laser sharp. It is just too easy these days to be distracted, and there is much at stake.

The next generation of homeschoolers is at stake.

"The most important [commandment]," answered Jesus, "is this: 'Hear, O Israel, the Lord our God, the Lord is one. Love the Lord your God with all your heart and with all your soul and with all your mind and with all your strength.' (Mark 12:28-30 ESV)

Did you hear that? Jesus said we MUST love the Lord God first. It is the most important command. Love God. Above all. Nothing else can come first –plain and simple. And loving Him means loving His ideals. It means following the standards that He has set for us.

Have we let the world's ideals take precedence over His? Are the world's standards becoming our standards? Are we trying to be like the world or like Him?

We need our lives to be based on one and only one ideal: God's standard. Instead, in our minds we have created impossible ideals based on worldly standards. We forget that God's Word trumps the Internet any day. God's Word has the answers we need and His standards are set there for us.

Before we jump on the Internet, do we search God's Word? Do we seek Him first? Do we pray? Or is our immediate instinct to search out social media? Are we searching out what everyone else has to say or are we searching out what God has to say?

When we get some quiet time, do we spend it online, or do we spend it with Him first?

Do we forget Who has called us to the homeschooling journey? Are we basing our ideals for our homeschools and our lives on the world's or His? Are we choosing Him first?

I Am Not Perfect, but My Savior Is...

I could answer all of these questions with the "wrong" answers. I've been there. I've done it. And that is why

I want to write about it and encourage others. I know the draw of the Internet…or the draw of asking everyone else before seeking God. I know the feeling of spending way too much time in the wrong places. I know the feeling of wanting approval from others. I know the tendency to fill up on "things" before the Word. Or making my house look "pretty" when my heart is pretty ugly.

I still fight. I have learned when I spend time at His feet and just listen, there is more peace and more clarity. I know when I spend time with Him first, He leads me and the desire to seek out other things dwindles. I am so far from perfect, but thankfully my Savior is perfect.

Those Pioneer Homeschoolers Did It Right…

We will be looking deep into the heart of homeschooling in this book. We'll delve into why we are doing what we do and how to avoid the distractions that tell us we should be focusing on things that don't have much lasting value. We will be resetting our focus if it has shifted off of Him and onto the world.

Years ago, before Pinterest and Facebook, before Instagram and all the other social media platforms, there were these pioneer homeschoolers –that first generation of families who answered a call. They didn't have the fancy curricula we have or the big homeschool conventions. They didn't have the networks we have of support groups and co-ops. They might not even have had any friends who were homeschoolers. And they didn't even have the Internet (gasp!). Homeschooling might have even been illegal where they lived. They did have, however, the most important thing.

Those early homeschoolers had a deep and strong conviction from the Lord to raise their children up at home, where they belonged. And because of those homeschoolers, we are here today.

The homeschooling movement has exploded because of those faithful first homeschooling families, the ones who were up against all odds but still followed His calling. We are here because of the ones who fully relied on God to lead them in this countercultural lifestyle. They had no idea what the future would hold for them, but they stepped out in faith.

I can only imagine the amount of time that they spent in prayer. I mean, here they were doing something virtually unheard of! Homeschooling was not at all like it is today. Not many people were doing it, and I am pretty sure that those who were homeschooling, were not looked at too favorably. They had faith to move mountains, and many mountains were moved indeed!

Imagine that kind of faith! I think we sometimes take for granted the homeschooling world of today. It wasn't always easy, accepted, or looked upon as "normal." It wasn't always an information-laden world with resources at our fingertips. My goodness, it wasn't even always legal! God called those early homeschoolers, and they obeyed, no matter what the cost.

The cost could have been ridicule, mockery, or even jail! We can't even fathom that these days. The focus wasn't on cutesy schoolrooms or getting the best curriculum. In reality, there was probably only ONE curriculum available to them! They moved forth in faith, raising their children with their strong convictions and their eyes fixed on the Lord's calling.

They didn't have all of the resources we have. They didn't have the ability to choose between mountains of curriculum catalogs or which vendors to visit at the homeschool conventions. They had one thing that they truly needed –His leading. And with Him leading, they have succeeded far beyond what they probably even thought was possible. The homeschooling movement has exploded, and we owe our ability to homeschool to those faithful pioneers. They paved the way for us.

Don't let their hard work have been in vain!

I think it is about time we go back to that mindset that tells us this homeschooling journey is not all about us but all about Him. It is not about proving anything to the world but obeying a call. It is about discipling our children in the ways of the Lord, and it is possible with a Bible and a prayer. We don't need the culture telling us we need to have a fancy schoolroom, elaborate curriculum, or perfection. He will work through our imperfections to make us beautiful –more beautiful than any worldly thing.

Have we become so wrapped up in portraying that perfect homeschooling family that we are more occupied with our image than with our hearts? Are we focused solely on academics so that spiritual needs are falling by the wayside? Are we filling up our schedules with endless activity, but neglecting time with Him? What are we truly teaching our children about our standards and Who sets them? Whose expectations are we trying to meet? His or the world's?

Are we basing our homeschool on a Pinterest board or Him?

Take a few minutes to ponder these questions. Journal your answers.

What are you basing your homeschool on? What are you basing your family's ideals on? Are they strictly built on the Word of God, or have you been basing it on what the world says is ideal?

Are you overwhelmed because you feel inadequate? Are you trying to keep up with the other families at co-op? Are you often distracted?

How do you define success in your homeschool? Is it based on what others say is success or what God says is success?

For our family, we know that if our children love the Lord with all their heart, soul, and mind, then we have achieved success. Because the truth is, if they are putting that into practice, all the rest will fall into place.

When you love God above all, you *can't* be unsuccessful in life...because Jesus says that is the MOST important.

I don't want to busy my life or my family's life with unimportant details. I want to be so busy running after God and following Him that I don't even have time to compare to what others are doing. That is truly success.

The real truth is that Pinterest and Instagram are a snapshot of a moment in time. And moments in time are not what we should be living for. God is. Standards based on others, and not on God, are not worth striving for.

Our standards come first and foremost from God's Word. What does God's Word say about how we are living? What does God's Word say about how we are raising our children? What does God's Word say our life should look like? What does God's Word say about our homes? Our parenting? Our stewardship? Our homeschools? What does His Word say about *all* we do?

Here are just a few things His Word does say. Take a few minutes to study the following verses:

Colossians 3:18-20 –Wives, submit yourselves to your husbands, as is fitting in the Lord. Husbands, love your wives and do not be harsh with them. Children, obey your parents in everything, for this pleases the Lord.

Ephesians 6:1-2 –Children, obey your parents in the Lord, for this is right. "Honor your father and mother"—which is the first commandment with a promise—

Ephesians 6:4 –Fathers, do not exasperate your children; instead, bring them up in the training and instruction of the Lord.

Psalm 127:3-5 –Children are a heritage from the Lord, offspring a reward from him. Like arrows in the hands of a warrior are children born in one's youth. Blessed is the man whose quiver is full of them. They will not be put to shame when they contend with their opponents in court.

Proverbs 1:8 –Listen, my son, to your father's instruction and do not forsake your mother's teaching.

Deuteronomy 6:6-9 –And these words that I command you today shall be on your heart. You shall teach them diligently to your children, and shall talk of them when you sit in your house, and when you walk by the way, and when you lie down, and when you rise. You shall bind them as a sign on your hand, and they shall be as frontlets between your eyes. You shall write them on the doorposts of your house and on your gates.

Romans 6:23 –For the wages of sin is death, but the free gift of God is eternal life in Christ Jesus our Lord.

Romans 12:2 –Do not be conformed to this world, but be transformed by the renewal of your mind, that by testing you may discern what is the will of God, what is good and acceptable and perfect.

Do Not Conform, But Be Transformed

When we keep up with His standards, we can cease striving to be like the world and be more like Him. When we use His Word as a guide, we don't have to rely on anything else. Our minds must be transformed and we must not conform.

I love how Romans 12:2 states this idea so clearly:

"Do not be conformed to this world, but be transformed by the renewal of your mind, that by testing you may discern what is the will of God, what is good and acceptable and perfect."

There you have it, right there. In a nutshell, that is a Real Homeschool: **one that is being transformed by God and following His perfect will while not being conformed to this world.**

When we let Him transform us, we won't conform to the world any longer. *We won't want to conform!* We want to have the mind of Christ, and that is done by letting Him change us. The more we seek Him and spend time in the Word, the more we become like Him. We stop chasing the world and we follow Him.

Keeping up with the wrong ideal can even become a competition. We have become a society that views those who have the most stuff as the most accomplished. Whoever throws the most adorable birthday party, complete with cutesy snacks and fancy decor, must be a good mom. Or whoever has the most elaborate lesson plans with creative crafts is the better teacher. At least, that is what the world makes us think.

We focus on the accessories as much as the children. We can't wait to show how we dress them, the toys we buy for them, and the rooms we decorate for them. We validate our parenting based on these ideals.

Our eyes are scanning one post to the next online, and they are all focused on material things. We can't help but have our minds filled with images. And those very images are difficult to get out of our minds. They become embedded in our minds as what our lives should be.

Somewhere along the way, our homeschools have started to follow this worldly pattern. The homeschooling movement went from a countercultural movement to blending right in with the world. We are showing off the good stuff. Dressing it up. Filling up with stuff. The focus has shifted off of the heart and onto how things look.

We are not being transformed anymore, but we are conforming to the world's ideals.

Don't get me wrong. We all want things to look nice. We all want to enjoy things. That is not the problem, in and of itself. The problem is *when we define our success and our worth by these things.* The problem comes when we compare our homeschool to others and when we start to doubt ourselves because of what everyone else is doing. The problem comes from focusing on the outside more than the inside.

And the biggest problem of all comes from these things distracting us from our first and foremost purpose in life: God Himself. And He alone is Who we answer to each day. We work for an audience of one.

Keeping up with the "Internet ideal" and not God's ideal will quickly be our downfall. We will end up striving for the world's approval and not His. We must remain vigilant in remaining true to God's standards. We are not called to look like the world but to look like disciples.

Has the homeschooling movement shifted away from its original spirit? Is it becoming more like the world? I don't know that it has yet, but I fear it might be moving in that direction. It has changed even since I started out ten years ago. And if it does move in that direction, I fear the next generation is in trouble. Instead of training our children in faith and with reliance on God, we might be training them to rely on the world.

Our homeschools should stand on strong faith and full reliance on God, just like those pioneer homeschoolers. If we keep looking to the world, we will end up quite confused and in an identity crisis. We will keep searching "for better" when His best is right there. He is all we need. It worked for those pioneers, and it can work for us.

Real Homeschool, at the heart, is getting back to that pioneer homeschool mindset. It is realizing the calling we have placed on our lives and not taking it lightly. We are raising the next generation to know Him and make Him known. We are training disciples for a hard and difficult world. We are not training disciples to fill up a cute Pinterest board. The calling is so much bigger than that.

Beginning each day with Him, rather than on the Internet is a start. Never let your eyes read something before you have read His Word first. I made this promise to myself years ago. I need to hear physically from Him before I start letting others cloud my mind. I must read His Word first in the morning before I scroll on my phone, check an email, or respond to a text. What we fill our minds with matters, folks! We must begin by filling our minds with Him. Then, we will have a little less room each day for the unimportant or useless noise.

I want my children to remember that I taught them about the Lord in our homeschool. I want them to remember that I gave them something very special. I gave them an education that focused on God and His Word. I want them to know Him above all else.

Teaching from the Bible is so simple, but we make it so complicated. We just need to open it and let it speak for itself. Even when it comes to Bible study, we can spend more time reading about *how to* study the Bible than we spend actually studying the Bible! God is sufficient enough to teach us if we let Him.

Sure, I can use all the help I can get from teachers and commentaries; but first and foremost, I need to listen to Him. He is sufficient.

All That Will Remain

I want my children to grow up to be God-honoring people who are on fire for the Lord. I need to be an example to them now and show them how that life looks. And the truth is, it is not found searching Pinterest. It is found in the Word, knowing Him, and getting out into the world, loving others and making Him known.

Life is too short to be spent chasing after an Internet-ideal life.

This homeschooling season will eventually end, and our children will grow up. Where are we storing our treasure? The material things we accumulate will not remain. Our packed schedules will not remain. The cutesy crafts will not remain.

What will remain in the hearts of our children? What are we investing in? Are we teaching them a lifelong love of God's Word? Are we teaching them eternal values?

The one thing that will remain is The Lord. Let us remember to store our treasure in heaven, and not here on earth. The world will pass away, but He will remain. Let our legacy for this generation be one that has taught them the Word, above all else.

Chapter 2

Real Life
What You See Isn't Necessarily the Full Picture

If Pinterest or Instagram pictures had sound, we might not all feel so inferior. We would probably hear the real deal going on in the background –the things that sound familiar in our own homes:

"Stop screaming."

"Don't argue with your sister."

"Sit still."

Several years ago, when I first started my blogging journey, I wrote a post titled "The Other Side of Homeschool." I wrote it after a conversation with a friend who was feeling badly for herself because her life never seemed to live up to the lives she had seen on the Internet. I told her that bloggers share selectively, and she had to take that into account. Just because they all look like they have it together doesn't mean they do. In fact, no one does all of the time.

As a blogger myself, I was also showing just one aspect of our life. I didn't want to be a complainer, so I rarely wrote "downer" posts. However, then it hit me. I needed to be real. I needed to show a real homeschool.

That week, as we were in the thick of one of our messiest homeschool weeks, I decided to document it and share online. I had a few sick kids at home, the house was a mess, and I was overwhelmed. I took a picture of the paint on the carpet that the two-year-old had spilled. I took a picture of my daughter's (messy) room. I even took a picture of the two-year-old in mid-tantrum wearing (mismatched) pajamas all day. Well, that post went viral. I guess it just really hit a nerve. People wanted to see "real." They wanted to know that they weren't alone after all. To this day, that post is my most viewed post ever on Simply Living…for Him.

Maybe I should have titled that post "The Real Side of Homeschool," instead of "The Other Side," because the truth is…I don't think it was the *other side* but actually the *real side.*

However, I didn't want to end that post with just showing our messes. I didn't want to leave it there; I wanted to give hope within the messy stuff. Ultimately, I showed how God worked through the messes and had redeemed each situation. That is what our God does. He cleanses us and is there to work with us through our rough spots. God can't come in to cleanse us and grow us if we have it all together already.

Cleaning Up for Company

Always remember that many bloggers and writers are just showing select parts of their life. There are many things that should be kept private, and rightfully so. They might not want to share all of their struggles and are willing to be transparent only in certain areas, and that is something to respect. You must remind yourself that writers usually write about a particular focus and not always every detail of their lives.

Be discerning with what you are reading. Glean from it what you can; but do not think you see the full picture, because when we think that is the full picture and start basing our ideal life on that (false) picture, we set ourselves up for trouble.

Sometimes we see a glimpse of people's lives–a moment in time that is frozen –and we judge their whole life based on that moment.

"Oh, they have the perfect family. The perfect home. The perfect (insert your own word here)"

However, if we realized that their life before that moment was nothing short of a deep pit from which they were rescued, so that now they wanted nothing more than to share the JOY of being rescued from that pit, we might think differently. Or if we knew that person had once lived in despair but now knows the TRUE joy of living a life for a Savior, we might see things differently. Or, perhaps that person had such a bad week that she is now rejoicing in that *one* good moment she did have.

Never be tempted to judge based on a moment. Share their joy. Share their moment. Don't internalize it in your life. Someone's moment has nothing to do with yours. Live your life rejoicing with others and sharing in others' joys. Build each other up. And work on making moments each day in your life.

Social media has brought a whole new level to relationships; don't let envy or bitterness or judgment take root. Be very discerning and guard your thoughts.

Social media is not necessarily real life. It is like dressing up and getting everything in order before the company comes over. When we have guests, we clean up everything just a little bit extra. We may even use our best dishes. Before the guests arrive, we lecture our kids about how to behave accordingly during the visit. Everyone smiles and is on his or her best behavior for that evening.

It isn't the full picture of what daily life looks like. And everyone knows that. When guests are over for dinner, they don't think your that life looks like the current picture 24 hours a day. That is why it took people by surprise when I published "The Other Side of Homeschool." Imagine showing up at my house for dinner as my toddler in his dirty and unmatched pajamas was throwing a tantrum? Picture us greeting you with our house in shambles with paint on the floor. It would seem strange.

Social media is often a showcase of the best of the best. Ever so slowly, we begin to idealize these showcases and set our standards based on them. We are setting our standards based on something other than God's Word.

These snapshots on social media have become something to strive for or something to attain. Birthday parties, weddings, showers, dinners parties, and even our homes are no longer sacred gatherings celebrating souls but instead have become a celebration of stuff. We are putting perfection on a pedestal. We are elevating *things* over *hearts,* the material over the spiritual. Everyone is trying to aspire to have their world look like that Pinterest post. But that is not reality.

Sure, Sally down the street has photos of her perfect devotional time while the kids have their hands folded and ears attentive. But did she have a photo of the minute devotions were over, and her son was giving attitude to her daughter? Maybe Mrs. Peters from co-op posted a picture on Facebook of her perfect homeschool room. Complete with a blackboard and matching bins from the designer store. But did she show you her kids sulking in the other room because she didn't want them to "mess it up?" All because she needed that pristine picture to post...

Which brings me to another difficult but real topic.

Stick with me for a minute here. Even if it makes you a bit uncomfortable, it needs to be said.

Dealing With Pride

We need to own up to our pride too –we all have been there. We are having a great moment, and we feel the need to "share it." We want everyone to know about it. Sometimes, I do just want to share my joy. There is nothing wrong with that. But it is a very fine line. I have learned always to check my motive first. Why am I sharing it? Is it with a spirit of pride? Is it just going to end up puffing me up for a bit?

Now we can't take responsibility if someone feels badly for our joy. That is certainly their issue. But we do need to be aware of causing others to stumble, and as I said, the most important issue is our heart motive.

Are we secretly searching for affirmation? My friends, do not seek affirmation from others, but from Him alone. That is where it matters.

Hard stuff. Really hard stuff. Stuff we need to face nonetheless. Head on. We can dance around these topics and continue to post away. But my fear is that social media isn't going away, and it is only going to evolve bigger and bigger. I can't imagine where it will be in just a few years. So these issues matter.

I will be touching on this more in the next chapter.

Remember, God looks at the heart. Nothing is hidden

from Him. If our hearts are deceitful (and we can even deceive ourselves), He knows it. Our focus must be on getting our hearts right with God first, before focusing on the outside; because really, the outside flows from the inside.

Chapter 3

Real Comparison
Avoiding the Comparison Trap.
You Work for An Audience of One

Since the beginning of time, we humans have struggled with comparison, envy, and coveting. With the explosion of social media, this problem has continued to grow. It is the perfect breeding ground for discontentment with what we have, and the yearning for what others have.

The truth is that the only thing we should be comparing to is Christ. He is our standard.

When we look at others, we take our eyes off the Lord and our goals. We start to let others set our standards and not Him.

What was meant to be helpful has quickly spun out of control into something that hinders us or even paralyzes us. Social media in and of itself is not evil, but some of the things that result from it can be. I think the original intentions of platforms such as Pinterest, Facebook, and Instagram were to share ideas and parts of our lives. They were a new way to form a sense of community and enhance communication. Of course, as with any good thing, our earthly selves can ruin it. We now have people who base their standards on these things, or they are consumed by them. There are others who are paralyzed by discontent from them or are just plain overwhelmed and distracted.

I truly believe homeschooling is a calling. It is a beautiful way to raise our children and a lifestyle that our family has enjoyed for almost ten years. I couldn't imagine doing anything else. That first year I began homeschooling, I was facing family opposition, pride, and insecurity from myself, not to mention I really had no idea what I was getting into! But the Lord did. He provided so much for me that year. He provided supernatural strength and courage. He provided just the right curriculum. I was really focused at that time on what HE wanted and not what I wanted, because the truth is, I never, ever, wanted to homeschool. But I knew He was calling me, so I put aside my fears and walked forth in faith.

I can only hope the Lord protected me in my first year of homeschooling in the sense that I did not have a Facebook account yet. There also was no such thing as Pinterest or Instagram back then. I can only imagine my scared little mama self, paralyzed by those things, because honestly, I could be easily paralyzed by own my fears already and didn't need anything else to add to them.

The funny thing is that first year, I am glad I was a little naive. I remember when a friend gave me her curriculum that she had finished for kindergarten. I thought, "Great, now I'm set." I had no inclination to look at anything else. Ha! I had no idea there were so many options, methods, styles, or even that there was an abundance of information out there. I just figured whatever she used would be sufficient. Oh, to still have that childlike faith!

And guess what? That curriculum would have been sufficient because God will work no matter what we choose, as long as we submit our whole selves to Him daily. Our homeschools, our lesson plans, our curriculum, and our families all should be laid at His feet, and we should trust Him to guide us. He has called us to homeschool and He will see it through. He didn't place this calling on our lives for us to do it in our own strength! He called us so that we can fully rely on Him.

I knew that God was calling me to homeschool, and I stepped out in faith, relying on Him to lead our family. I didn't look too far ahead. If I had gone over all of the things that could fail, I probably never would have started. If I had asked, "What if?" I probably never would have started. If I had relied on myself, I definitely never would have started.

I said we would try homeschooling for just one year, or until God told us to stop. I didn't have much of a plan except to obey God's call. It was a leap of faith and a complete reliance on God.

However, the next few years in my homeschooling journey brought about the explosion of social media. All of a sudden, there was an exponential amount of information available at my fingertips. I started to realize there was more than that one curriculum. There was a whole community of homeschoolers out there, and many of them were sharing their information online!

I would spend hours searching the Internet looking for the best curriculum. I had good intentions, but I was also getting distracted by the blogs and Facebook posts. Everyone else seemed to have this journey down pat. I was not feeling adequate at all. It was disheartening. My homeschool did not look like the homeschools that were online.

The curriculum choices were beyond overwhelming. I would search endlessly, comparing each one to the next. I am ashamed at how much time I spent *away from my kids* because I was searching the internet. I am even more ashamed that I spent that time *away from God.*

Imagine the amount of time I spent comparing to others and comparing curriculum, when I could have been seeking God. I could have prayed and read my Bible and spent time at His feet! I wasn't seeking Him, but I was seeking others. I was looking to the world for answers before I turned to Him.

God looks at the heart. He wants us to raise our children up with His Word. He wants us to raise them to fulfill spiritual desires, not desires of the flesh. He doesn't want us looking for answers on the Internet or from others, but in Him first. Sure, we can find great ideas on there to help us, but we should never think we will find all of the answers on there alone. Once we have sought His guidance (then and only then) should we turn to others for guidance.

I don't believe that God wants us chasing after the worldly model of filling up on material and mental clutter. He doesn't want us doing this in our own strength. And He certainly doesn't want us relying on other people or things to get the job done.

Your Homeschool Shouldn't Look Like My Homeschool

In all honesty, your homeschool shouldn't look like mine. Everyone has a different purpose that God has ordained for each family. It's like comparing apples and oranges. No two homeschools are the same. He has called each of us for a unique purpose, and that is quite exciting!

The comparison trap holds you hostage and keeps you focused on an idealized homeschool. It keeps you focused on yourself, which is never a good thing. You want it all to be perfect, and you don't want to have any messes. Have you forgotten that God often works through those messes?

Perhaps your family is struggling. Perhaps no one is participating in devotions, or your tenth-grader just can't get Algebra. Maybe your eight-year-old still can't read. And maybe, just maybe, God is teaching you through those situations. Maybe He has you in those situations so that you will struggle through it as a family and grow together.

How will we (or our kids) learn if we don't go through tough times? Nothing worth doing is ever easy, and we don't learn unless we work. You have the responsibility to help your children get through those difficulties.

Sometimes that means asking for help from others and seeking advice from mentors. God gives us all kinds of people in our lives just for those purposes. But there is a difference between seeking advice and coveting what someone else is doing. When you compare yourself to another person and then feel self-pity, that becomes the comparison trap.

Since we only see snippets of people's lives online, we will then take each of those snippets and blend them into one perfect homeschool. That doesn't exist. Instead, it is a compilation of a person's (or several people's) best. In reality, each of us has some showcase moments, and each of us has those behind-the-scenes moments, and God is in all of them.

We Are Running a Marathon Together

Homeschool is *not* a competition –it a serious calling from the Lord and a very personal decision between you and the Lord. It is about God's purpose being unveiled for *your* family, that is unique to your family. We are not running a race against each other but a marathon alongside each other, for a common goal. We want to honor the Lord.

God isn't going to compare what we are doing to others. *He* sets the standard. So take your eyes off of what everyone else is doing, and focus your gaze onto what God wants for you.

Maybe you have no idea what God wants for your family. Maybe it is because you have been distracted for too long with what everyone else is doing or how you think the ideal homeschool should look. Maybe it's because you haven't even asked Him yet.

Take some time with Him alone.
Truly alone and unplugged.
Ask Him.
Seek Him.
Then follow Him.

Take the time to really get into the Word and let Him speak to you through it. Study it. Pray, and pray some more about the goals for your family. The exciting thing is that your family goals are unique! We are not carbon copies of other families. What defines success for one family does not define success for yours! Isn't that freeing?

Do Not Covet

The comparison trap is a serious issue. Not only are we comparing to others, we can also begin to covet. We are breaking a commandment when we look at someone else's life or homeschool (or whatever it is) and want it for ourselves. Sometimes, we even secretly hope the other person fails because, in some warped way, it makes us feel better about ourselves. It is all sinful thinking.

It can start as admiration and then quietly creep into envy, and before long you are rejecting what you have because you want what someone else has. That is sin, and we need to deal with that sin.

When you compare your family to another family, you are telling God that you aren't happy with the blessings He has given you in your family. You are saying He has given someone else something better than what He has given you. That is a path we should never travel.

What causes quarrels and what causes fights among you? Is it not this, that your passions are at war within you? You desire and do not have, so you murder. You covet and cannot obtain, so you fight and quarrel. You do not have, because you do not ask. You ask and do not receive, because you ask wrongly, to spend it on your passions. You adulterous people! Do you not know that friendship with the world is enmity with God? Therefore whoever wishes to be a friend of the world makes himself an enemy of God (James 4:1-4 ESV).

We talked about how we see snippets of someone's day on social media. I also want to point out that we see also a snippet of their *entire life.* We don't know the whole history of what has brought a person to where he or she is today. And it matters because we are comparing ourselves to just a snippet.

An Instagram Photo Is Merely a Moment In a Roller-Coaster Life

Have you ever considered a time from your past and realized it does not accurately represent the "totality" of you? For instance, I am not the person I was 20 years ago. In fact, I am 180 degrees different from who I was then. I wasn't walking with the Lord. I was fully rebelling, and I had surrounded myself with people who weren't beneficial for me. I was a mess. I was in despair. It wasn't a pretty picture. Trust me, you would be shocked.

So, fast forward to my life now, which is full of so much work that God has done, and I can't help but share it sometimes! I have so much joy when I see how far He has brought me.

Now suppose someone has no idea of my past, and has no idea what I have been through, and just sees what I post today, which is merely one moment in a long life of ups and downs. This person doesn't know the feeling I have when I post that beautiful sunrise from my home…how I always dreamed of a day when I'd live somewhere with that view, instead of living in an apartment above a deli in the city, lost in utter darkness. The casual reader doesn't know my mindset or my motive when I post those pictures of my kids… because there once was a day when I thought I might never fulfill my dream of becoming a mom. This person can't sense my underlying feelings when I talk about my husband doing something nice for me, because there was once a day when the only "love" I knew was from a boyfriend who abused me.

I want to give glory for all the Lord has done. The truth is, He has amazed me with all that He has worked in my life, and I can't help but share His work and my joy. My life is nothing short of a miracle, and He deserves the credit for every bit of it.

Do you see things in a different light now? When we judge someone else's life now, we don't always have the full picture. We need to be very careful not to judge the motive or lives of others. We only see what we are presented in that moment. And comparing your own full reality –encompassing the beauty *and* the messes– to those small snippets just doesn't make any sense. It has nothing to do with your own life. Take it for what it is –a pretty picture –and move on.

The heart is deceitful above all things, and desperately sick; who can understand it (Jeremiah 17:9 ESV)?

Beware of Judgment

We are to be very careful when we judge another's heart. We can never know someone else's true heart; only God can. We might think we know or have things figured out –but really, that is pride. Our judgment of others is really pride in us. We think we have it down pat, so we scorn what another is doing. Ha! All of our hearts are deceitful, mine being the worst. God is the only one who knows a true heart. Whenever we feel the need to judge another's heart, we should begin with ourselves. If we are right with God, we will not be looking to point out others' flaws. That's God's job. Seek Him first. Seek His approval and not man's.

Chapter 4

Real Priorities
No Idolatry

A homeschool should never become an idol. Homeschooling is a lifestyle, but it is not our whole life. We don't define ourselves by being homeschoolers but by being children of God. Our identity rests in Him.

For a while during my homeschooling journey, I fell into the trap of trying to define myself by my homeschooling. I thought that since this was my calling, it was also my identity. No. God has called me to be His child, and that is where my identity lies.

Too often we become so consumed with our homeschool that we forget that we should be consumed by Him. Instead of filling up our homeschool with more books, games, gadgets, and decor, we should fill it with the love, joy, and peace that come from Him alone. We are teaching our children about Him every day through our homeschool.

We should be looking to Him and not to what Pinterest says is perfect or what others say is ideal. Our homes should be built on Him, decorated with His love, adorned with His grace. All the fancy decor in the world cannot be more beautiful than a home filled with God's love and grace.

We are teaching our children how to relate to each other as God tells us we should…on the good days and the bad. We are training them and discipling them. We should be teaching them His Word and pointing to Him in all things.

Give Me The T-Shirt and Bumper Sticker–I'm a Homeschooler!

At one point I thought I needed my home to scream "We homeschool!" I wanted the t-shirt, the bumper sticker –anything that would let people know *I was a homeschooler!* Perhaps I thought it validated my decision. Perhaps I thought it made me feel important. Who knows? But I do know that it was the wrong heart attitude. It was focused on what the outside looked like without much attention to the inside. I wanted the world to know *we were homeschoolers…*but did they know, most importantly, that we were disciples of Christ? That is where our true identity lies: n*ot in what we do, but in who He is.*

We need to stop screaming about what we do and start shouting about WHO HE IS! Let our lives reflect Him and Him alone. Homeschool can be a part of that, but ultimately it is a small part. Our identity lies in so much more than being homeschoolers. We are mothers, daughters, wives, friends, teachers, and so much more. First and foremost, we are daughters of a King! Let our lives show that. Let us reflect Him. Let us radiate His love!

Unfortunately, I was teaching my children that we should look the part of the "good homeschoolers." We should have that perfect homeschooler house and behave in a certain way. I might not have told them that in so many words, but my actions surely communicated that message.

The truth is, our children are watching us and our behavior. If my focus is on how things look, it sends a strong message to them. Unfortunately, it is the wrong message.

I wanted the perfect "school room" with maps on the walls, a globe in the corner, educational posters, and lots and lots of books! I wanted my children to be above average in academics because "good" homeschoolers were always ahead and always seemed so smart! After all, I wanted to make sure we *looked like* successful homeschoolers!

Ha! Success? What is success?

True Success

I have often said, "What does it matter if my children know all the facts in the world but don't know Him? So what if they can read, but they don't read the Word?"

Call me an underachiever, but what does it matter to be successful in the world's eyes, but not God's? Who defines success? I may be an underachiever by the world's standards, but I am not looking for worldly achievement. I aim to make disciples –and that, my friends, is eternal gain.

We are making disciples. Our homeschool is not a perfect picture, because it is a training ground for our children (which can get messy!) and that training ground begins with their hearts.

The inside is where it all begins. We should be so consumed with Him that we don't even notice what appearances are. In truth, when we are filled with Him, our outward appearance will be more beautiful to others than we can imagine, because they will see a true and authentic godly mom, following Him and raising her children in the Lord. No amount of schoolbooks lining the shelves, maps on the wall, or dressed-up school rooms can compare to that!

Are we idolizing academics? Or are we idolizing Him? Superior academics will not make superior disciples. That is not to say we can't have both. We can. We need to focus on the discipleship part first, however.

I truly believe when we put God first, He will supply all of our needs, just as Matthew 6:33 states. If He wants my children to obtain great academic achievements, then He will see it through. Our job is to seek first His righteousness. My heart needs to be open to wherever He leads us. Making disciples is my first and foremost job. If I start to focus on the academic part of homeschooling above the spiritual part, I am raising really knowledgeable kids, but not necessarily wise ones.

God's wisdom is far superior to any earthly knowledge. And while knowledge is important, it means nothing if I haven't taught my children to love the Lord above all else. If they aren't putting God first, when they grow up they will not be properly equipped for life, regardless of their SAT scores. Just remember: a degree from an Ivy League college does not make a disciple, yet a disciple can certainly have a degree from an Ivy League college. Make sense?

Chapter 5

Real Training Ground

Life is Our Classroom- Beyond the Four Walls Of a Picture-Perfect Room

Homeschooling is about so much more than a classroom. Nowadays everyone seems to want to share that perfect homeschool room. When on earth did we decide this is important? Life is our classroom. We are teaching our children so much more than what we confine within the walls of a classroom. We spend hours upon hours creating that perfect homeschool room and then taking pictures of it to share online. Our focus shouldn't be on a classroom.

Our focus should be teaching our children that homeschooling is about lifelong learning and attaining godly wisdom. Yet, we are teaching them that the room needs to look a certain way, or we won't be successful. I bet some of the best lessons learned were never inside of those four walls with the matching pillows and couches. I bet the best lessons learned have nothing to do with how the homeschool room looked. And the best lessons learned were in real life, not in a picture-perfect schoolroom.

I cringe when I see the pictures floating around the Internet showing classrooms in our houses. While it can be fun and exciting to decorate, may it not consume us. I used to be consumed by it. I would fret because we didn't have the space to re-create some of those beautiful learning spaces I saw online. I would start to feel a little bit of envy deep down. I would look at my house, which God had provided as a blessing for us, and feel discontentment.

I thought if I had more space or a better layout, or a better system in place, then our homeschool would run more smoothly. I never thought maybe I should start praying for smoother days first. I thought if I had better organization supplies, we would be more successful. I never thought perhaps success started in my heart, and not in the house.

God will provide success in our homeschool regardless of the room we have or the decor we use. Can we limit His ability to work? At one time, I did. I focused on me and what I was doing, rather than what He could do. I was focused on the outside, not necessarily the inside. I had put God in a box, and that box was literally those classroom walls. God is so much bigger than that! Don't limit His ability. He does not need a picture-perfect room to work through us and our homeschools.

The Best Lessons Learned Are in the Classroom Called "Life"

When I changed perspectives and truly let Him lead us, it transformed us. When I realized that God wanted to work in my heart and not my house, I was free from worldly ideals and I started seeking His ideals. No longer was I scanning the Internet for ideas or methods or purpose, but I was taking my concerns quietly to Him in prayer. He started answering those prayers in ways I hadn't anticipated.

Suddenly I saw the lessons He provided us, and they usually had nothing to do with how our house looked or even what curriculum we used. In fact, our best year of homeschooling took place the year that we used practically *no* curriculum and had no budget. That year, my husband had been laid off and we were financially unstable. We used the Bible as our main textbook. That year He was our Master Teacher, and we depended on Him for everything.

Some of the lessons we learned that year were never planned, yet they are the ones that most likely will stick with my children forever. We learned to rely on God for everything. We learned what constant prayer and focus on Him really looked like. And guess what? We didn't have the distractions of trying to decorate or to fill up with material items because it wasn't in the budget. Once that option was removed from my life, it actually freed me up from focusing on things that we really didn't *need.* I could not afford to buy anything for our school room or to decorate, and all of those fancy classrooms weren't even an option anymore. Many distractions had been taken away from me, which was actually proved to be a blessing.

It changed everything that year. I saw firsthand that God will teach us, when we step aside to let Him do the teaching. So many intimate times with Lord were spent that year that I often have to remind myself of that time in our lives. How soon I can forget.

I can be just like the Israelites. He provided for us, and then as soon as we pass through the waters, I am grumbling again. I have to remember that we did it that year with no extras –just relying on Him and His Word. So even now, when I start to get distracted, I remind myself of that year.

God wants to teach our children, and He teaches us outside of a classroom daily. We can just be outside and learn hundreds of things about Him. Nature constantly screams His name. His character is evident everywhere.

Look at the birds, the flowers, and the insects, each so intricately made. They scream His name.

Look at the rainbows, the clouds, and the ocean. He is vast and majestic. He is powerful and creative and every other word you can think of to describe Him! There aren't even enough words!

He also teaches us through so many real-life situations. Our kids are constantly able to learn about real life as homeschoolers because they live in the real world every single day. They can be part of so much of our lives when not confined to a classroom. So why do we try to re-create one in our homes?

As I said, I did this. We set up a school room at home and decorated it. I know. It's fun. There's nothing wrong with that in itself. It's cute. I get it! The problem comes in when we focus on it too much. I saw firsthand that it didn't teach my children much about God's Word. A mommy focused on decorating a schoolroom is not what I want them to remember. I want them to remember that I taught them about God and who He is above all. I want them to know His ways and not the world's ways. I want them to see He works in our lives regardless of the circumstances.

Chapter 6

Real Messes

There is Beauty in the Mess

God works through our messes. We can feel free to admit our messes, but the beauty is that we don't have to leave them there. We can let Him help us clean them up.

Sometimes life is just plain messy, and that's okay because that is where God can really work. In fact, it is the messiest times in which we often learn the most through a deep cleansing. Why are we so afraid to let others see those messes? As Christians, and brothers and sisters in Christ, we should allow each other to see the messes for a few reasons:

- It allows others to help us, giving them an opportunity to serve us and minister to us. We are to help build each other up and carry each other's burdens.

- It also allows us to be real enough and authentic enough with others, which in turn creates the intimate relationships we should be having. Real is always best. If we can't be real with each other, then the relationship is based on superficiality.

Messes aren't something to be ashamed of. In fact, the only time we should be ashamed of them is when we leave them there. There is a story in the mess. Seeing all things redeemed and seeing how God works in the worst of times is a beautiful thing to witness.

Instagram lets us filter our lives. Add that little bit of faded background or that tinted color, and we have the feeling of peace or joy. In life we can't add a filter to change the truth. We need to be transparent right there for all to see.

Life Unfiltered

We need to be real with each other, unfiltered. Those are the true and authentic relationships that last through all of the ups and downs of our lives.

The best friends I have are the ones who can come over unannounced, that I never feel I have to clean up for…because they know me and my heart. I don't feel judged if the tables are dusty or there are still dishes in the sink. I enjoy going to people's houses that are like that…because the pressure is off. It's like the masks are off, and the inside shines rather than the outside.

Messes are part of life. As I have said, though, we shouldn't have a complain-fest or wallow in our messes; rather we should be available to others to help them through the messes.

God wants to work in us. We can't pretend with Him. He knows every mess, and He will be there to help us work through each one.

We have had some pretty messy years. We've had job losses; I've dealt with anxiety; we've had health scares and death in the family. We even moved to a new town. All of these situations are so imperfect; but still, God taught us in each situation.

If everything were perfect all the time, we wouldn't need a Savior!

Laugh, Pray, and Cry with Each Other

I recently met with a group of women, some of whom I hadn't seen in a very long time. A few I didn't really know all too well, except for a wave at the grocery store or a brief conversation at the co-op. I was completely astounded when one of them revealed she was struggling with depression.

I mean, this is the type of woman that you *always* see smiling. She seems to radiate happiness. I was completely shocked when she stated it is hard for her to get out of bed some days.

As we talked, guess what happened? The tears flowed as each of us said we had been there –some maybe not as severely depressed, and some even more depressed. Every woman in the room shook her head in agreement, though, tears flowing.

In that moment I was sure more than ever that we need to be real. The connection we all had made knowing we had all been there and *admitting* to it, was like a glimpse of heaven. There are no constraints. We all connected on a level that rarely occurs in everyday life.

We were being real: our true selves, the ones that we often try to hide for fear of being judged, or for fear of not looking like a Pinterest-perfect mom, were out in the open. The weight of the world was lifted, and God was doing the lifting.

Then we prayed together.

What a beautiful moment when souls unite because of Jesus. What a beautiful moment when we stop pretending we have it all together and unite with each other. What a beautiful moment when women are real.

Be real. Let others in when it's messy. Don't apologize for it. We all fall short, and we all can admit our flaws because the foot of the cross is equal ground for us all.

Be real in the mess. We need each other. We need Him.

Chapter 7

Real Homeschool
Join the Movement

Now that we have truly searched our hearts and placed our eyes back where they belong, will you join me in a movement to lift each other up and lock arms on this journey together? Will you join me as we go about our daily life, encouraging one another and building each other up? Let's be real.

When that mom you've run into in the grocery store asks, "How's it going?" don't answer, "Oh, great!" and proceed to pick out only the good parts of life. It is truly okay to say, "Well, I've been struggling and could use some prayer." On the flipside, don't hesitate to be the mom who puts out her hand, and prays for her friend...right there in the grocery store.

Or, if you see someone who is struggling, drop her a note and tell her that you are praying for her. Stop over and offer to hang out with her kids while she grabs a cup of coffee alone. Whatever it is, instead of everyone trying to mask their true selves and live up to everyone else's image, let's *be real.*

Let your friends know your house doesn't always sparkle. Let them know last night you all had cereal for dinner. I promise relationships will be stronger when we are real.

And let us consider how to stir up one another to love and good works, not neglecting to meet together, as is the habit of some, but encouraging one another, and all the more as you see the Day drawing near. (Hebrews 10:24-25 ESV)

And remember to rejoice with those who rejoice! This is so important. If someone is sharing a beautiful moment, rejoice with her! If someone is sharing a great homeschool day, rejoice with her! If someone is sharing a joyous moment, share the joy with her! Don't hold in bitterness or let envy take root. Rejoice with your sisters.

On that note, when someone is weeping over a struggle, weep with her. And then walk beside her, gently holding their hand as a sister in Christ, and gently lift her back up.

Don't Do Life Alone

We need each other. God made us for relationships – but good, healthy, and pure relationships, not the kind you find in the world, often laced with jealousy and hypocrisy. Develop the ones that have a pure motive, that are never self-seeking; and always have the other person's interests above your own.

And remember…we don't want to have a complain-fest either. We are free to talk about our struggles, knowing that God (and our best girlfriends) are there to help us work through the messes but not to leave them there. So instead of throwing everything in a closet when company comes over, leave it out, but ask for help cleaning it up, if needed.

We also must go back to real and authentic relationships –where we see the good, the bad, and the ugly –the ones where we don't compete with each other, but we link arms with each other. We walk together, hand in hand, letting the Lord lead our steps. Will you join me?

We must hold each other accountable and we can begin with ourselves. Make sure we put His Word above all others' words. Get together with your friends and study the Bible together, pray together, and seek Him together. Encourage one another just like it tells us to in the Bible.

If we are all seeking Him together, the world won't look so appealing anymore. We will walk together, seeking Him as sisters, thirsting for Him more. Isn't that a beautiful picture? It's prettier than anything you will ever see on Pinterest and certainly much more ideal than a filtered Instagram picture.

Join me. Sure, you can share what you've learned in this book online…I'd love for you to spread the word! **But mostly I want you to get out there in real life.**

Really live.

Live a *real* life with others in the real world –a life that aspires to God's ideal but acknowledges imperfection… and that leans heavily on God and your sisters in Christ to grow despite the messes. The truth is, until we get to Glory, we will never have the Pinterest-perfect or the Instagram-ideal life, but oh, in Glory it will never even compare to anything we have ever seen on this earth.

I can't wait for that moment, can you? When heaven is revealed to be more beautiful than anything we have imagined. Yet, while we are here, we can create little glimpses of heaven here on earth, by knowing Him and making Him known. Share Him with a hurting world. Love on others, with true and authentic love.

Let the world know about His ideals and His standards. Reflect His love. That will be the best thing you could ever share..far above any Internet post. *Yes, share His love.*

Be real, sisters. Be so, so real. It matters. It matters in life and in our homeschools. It all begins in the home, and then it spills out into this world. Let's make sure we are representing Him well. We are ambassadors of Christ. Live like it.

About Karen DeBeus:

Karen was called to homeschool when her oldest child was about to enter kindergarten. She had no intention of homeschooling; after trying to run as far as she could from it, she obeyed the call and is now passionate about homeschooling. Karen is the author of Simply Homeschool, Called Home, and Real Homeschool. She speaks nationally at homeschool events, and truly believes her ministry is to encourage others on their journey.

Karen is also the author of her blog Simply Living for Him, and she is the owner of Bible Based Homeschooling.

To find out more, please visit Simply Living for Him.

Karen loves to speak with other families and can be reached via email at karen@simplylivingforhim.com.

20 Ways to Keep It Real Right Now

1. **Invite a friend over for coffee, spontaneously, and leave your house just the way it is.** Focus on relationships and not things. Don't try to impress with the perfect house. A listening ear or a good laugh (or cry!) is so much more meaningful. Fight the urge to make everything perfect –be real.

2. **Start a moms prayer group.** Meet weekly at the park when the weather is warm. The kids can play while the moms pray. We used to do this, and I called it, Pray & Play Day.

3. **Commit to reading God's Word before anything else each morning.** This is a discipline that will reap far more benefits than you can imagine! What we fill our mind with matters.

4. **Offer to watch another mom's kids just because**. Perhaps that mom just needs to be home. Alone. Taking her kids, even for an hour, may help her reset and refocus. Be a blessing. In return, you will be blessed.

5. **Take an Internet fast.** Every time you feel the need to "check in" online, check in with God. He is right there waiting for you all the time. So often we turn to see what others are doing or tell others what we are doing. Spend that time with the Lord instead.

6. **Post a picture online without staging it just so.** Let others know that you are keeping it real!

7. **Ask for help.** Do not be ashamed to call a friend to ask for prayer, or even if she can take your kids for an hour or two. We need to reach out; we aren't meant to struggle alone. Chances are, your friends need you as much as you need them.

8. **When tempted to wallow in self-pity because your homeschool doesn't look like another's, remind yourself it is not supposed to look like anyone else's.** Immediately start a list of what God is doing in *your* homeschool. Keep your focus where it needs to be. Then ask Him to show you where you can improve or what He wants for your family. Then follow Him. Trust Him. He will lead you.

9. **Keep a gratitude journal.** Refer to it often when you are feeling discouraged. Most likely, you will see you have far more blessings than you thought.

10. **Start an accountability group.** Gather a few girlfriends and promise to keep it real with each other. Call them when you feel you are struggling.

11. **Have that same accountability group help keep you accountable for online time.** When you see each other online too much, remind each other where your hearts need to be. Take it a step further, and keep a log of time spent online; if you are lacking the self-control, this log will help you recognize if your online time is getting to be excessive.

12. **Resist the urge to post every picture and every memory.** Keep some just for your family. Not everything needs to be shared.

13. **Ditch the curriculum catalogs.** If you are happy with your curriculum, don't look at any others, no matter how great someone else insists they are. If your curriculum is working for you, stick with it. The less

clutter, the more likely you are to stay focused.

14. **Resist the urge to say yes to every extracurricular activity out there.** Yes, we want our kids to be "well-rounded"–isn't that the excuse we always use?– If it is causing you stress, it is not bearing fruit. Only choose things that are truly beneficial; avoid making choices for the sake of trying to look busy or keep up with anyone else.

15. **Have cereal for dinner sometimes.** Really. It's okay. Not every meal has to look like a Pinterest recipe. Kids just want to eat! And hey, every once in a while, cereal is a fun alternative.

16. **Stop working on the homeschool room.** If you have a designated space to keep everything, that sure helps with organization, but don't fret over the details. Don't think it has to be pretty to be successful. A plastic bin serves the same function as a pretty basket from the designer store. God cares what our children's hearts look like, not what the homeschool room looks like.

17. **Own up to your mistakes.** Say you're sorry. When kids see that even mom makes mistakes, they will learn how to take responsibility for their own mistakes. Let them see your need for a Savior. Let them know that no one is perfect. We all need a Savior.

18. **Cultivate a thirst for eternal and not material treasures.** There is much more value in those things! Start by getting rid of physical clutter that is causing you stress. Simplify, simplify, simplify!

19. **Join the movement.** Will you share with your homeschool community the need to be real? It is actually contagious. When others see someone who is real and down to earth, they are drawn to them. We all crave it. So be it. Invite others on the journey with you. Use the hashtag #RealHomeschool in your media. Let the world know, we are taking off our facades and living life *real.*

20. **Share this book with another friend.** Let the need to be real spread throughout the homeschooling community. Let's get back to *God.* Let's ditch the perfect, for *His* perfect.

Connect with other real moms at
www.facebook.com/realhomeschool
or www.thereahomeschool.com

#RealHomeschool

TRANSFORMATION BEGINS WITH HIM

The biggest way to transform your thoughts and your life, is to get in His Word.

Take some time to see what the Lord has to say about how you should live, before seeking out what the Internet has to say.

We often say we have no time for the Word, but we spend endless hours searching the Internet, reading articles and blogs, and scanning social media. Make use of your time wisely. Spend it with Him first!

Look for verses on the following:

1. Raising children

Verses:_____

Application:_____

_____

_____

2. Practicing Hospitality

Verses:_____

Application:_____

_____

_____

3. Eternal Perspective

Verses:_____

Application:_____

_____

4. Humility

Verses:_____

Application:_____

_____

_____

5. Friendships

Verses:_____

Application:_____

_____

_____

6. Coveting

Verses:_____

Application:_____

_____

_____

7. Prayer Life

Verses:_____

Application:_____

_____

_____

8. Where Our Treasure Lies

Verses:_____

Application:_____

_____

_____

9. Pride

Verses:_____

Application:_____

_____

_____

10. Honesty

Verses:_____

Application:_____
_____
_____

Take time to write down any other ways God is teaching you in His Word. Let this practice take precedence over searching out other things. Seek Him first!

A Prayer for a Real Homeschool

Dear Lord,

Let me honor You in all of my ways.

Let me teach my children about You first.

Let me teach them that You are to be known above any earthly thing.

Let me create a home that is filled with love, joy, peace, and faithfulness before I fill it with material treasures.

Let me practice humility daily and serve my family and others out of love.

Let me find kindred sisters who will walk with me.

Let me remember that my homeschool belongs to You, and You are ultimately in charge.

Let me remember that this world is passing away, and I will take no earthly treasure with me, but the treasures I am storing in heaven matter most.

Let me be real with my family, my friends, and a watching world.

Help me to use my time wisely and not fill it up with useless tasks and endless searching for earthly treasures.

Let me do all things for Your glory and not the glory of others.

Let me rely solely on You –when the budget is tight, the days are long, and hard times come –let me remember that You will supply the strength and provision we need.

Let me walk this journey knowing I aim to impress no one, but that I may please You alone in all of my ways.

Let me remember You called me to this journey, and this journey is all about You.

Amen.

Made in the USA
Coppell, TX
17 March 2020

17063520R00049